This bite-sized book  an overview of how will help you to:

- Understand the value of building a culture of wellbeing
- Support people through volatility, disruption and uncertainty
- Promote positivity and eliminate toxic influences
- Lead with compassion and empathy to build trust
- Help people find meaning and purpose in what they do
- Be a role model and set a great example

We are embedding health and wellbeing at the heart of our business strategy because our people are our greatest asset

Alex Gourlay

Building a culture of wellbeing

Healthy, happy and productive people are at the very heart of every successful and sustainable organisation. There is a growing appreciation of the link between wellbeing and productivity and the importance of building and supporting a positive culture. There is also an increasing amount of compelling evidence that demonstrates an impressive return on investment for those organisations which invest in the wellbeing of their people.

On this basis, employee wellbeing is now one of the key focuses for leaders and human resource management practitioners. Leaders need to ensure that employees are supported with resources, tools and on-site healthcare opportunities to fully support the overall wellbeing of their people.

Speed, agility and
responsiveness are the
keys to future success

Anita Roddick

Are your people fit for the future?

We are living in unprecedented and unpredictable times and it can be disruptive and challenging. Not only have we experienced a global pandemic, the fourth industrial revolution is upon us and is evolving exponentially. Disruption is rife in almost every industry all over the world and these changes herald huge transformation.

This is a revolution that will change the way we live, work and relate to one another, and is unlike anything we have experienced before, simply because the speed of the current breakthroughs has no historical precedent. Ensuring that employees are fit for the future will depend a great deal on their overall wellbeing and the support they receive.

READY FOR ANYTHING?

Living in a VUCA world

The world is always changing. However, every now and again, there are times in history where all the forces of change seem to come together to produce an era-defining shift.

VUCA is an acronym that was first used in 1987, based on the leadership theories of Warren Bennis and Burt Nanus, and a term used in military vocabulary. It describes a world of volatility, uncertainty, complexity and ambiguity and its relevance has never been felt and experienced as much as it is today.

Thriving in a VUCA world

A counteract for VUCA is known as VUCA Prime. VUCA Prime is a behavioural leadership model that was first introduced in 2007 by Bob Johansen, who is a distinguished fellow at the Institute for the Future. This model helps leaders to focus on four key elements of modern leadership as follows:

- Vision rises above volatility and when conditions are changing unpredictably, leaders need to keep people focused on the end goal
- Understanding reduces anxiety around uncertainty and provides an opportunity for exploration and learning
- Clarity counters complexity and simplifies things to keep people better informed so they can be more decisive and productive
- Agility overcomes ambiguity and enables people to adapt quickly and easily

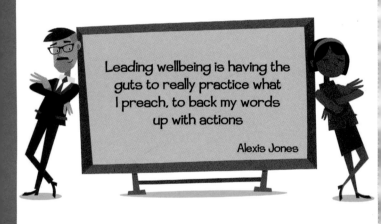

Leading wellbeing is having the guts to really practice what I preach, to back my words up with actions

Alexis Jones

What is wellbeing?

Wellbeing can be described as the experience of health, happiness and prosperity. This includes having good mental and physical health, the ability to manage stress levels, a sense of purpose and high life satisfaction. In a nutshell, wellbeing is about living as well as we possibly can.

Wellbeing is also a core enabler of employee engagement and organisational performance. Supporting wellbeing at work can prevent stress, help people achieve a better life balance and create positive working environments, where individuals and organisations can thrive.

Leading Wellbeing

The seven wisdoms of wellbeing

Spiritual wellbeing

Emotional wellbeing

Physical wellbeing

Social wellbeing

Financial wellbeing

Digital wellbeing

Environmental wellbeing

© Liggy Webb

The holistic approach to wellbeing

There are many components to wellbeing and the real wisdom is the consideration and practical application of each of the following:

Emotional wellbeing - constructively channelling emotions to maintain positive mental health

Physical wellbeing - combining healthy eating, exercise, relaxation and sleep to manage energy and stress levels and support immunity

Social wellbeing - feeling included and connected

Financial wellbeing - being able to make informed choices to enjoy life, both now and in retirement

Digital wellbeing - managing the influences and impact of technologies and digital services

Environmental wellbeing - occupying a healthy, enjoyable and stimulating environment

Spiritual wellbeing - finding meaning and purpose

How
to lead
wellbeing

Equip people to do their job

Before you can even begin to think about implementing any additional wellbeing support, it is essential that you equip people with the tools to be able to do their job. Technology can often be a barrier and so ensuring people have the equipment and support they need is essential.

It is also important to establish that the environment people are working in is conducive to wellbeing. When your team are working remotely, this can be a bit more challenging to manage and so opening the conversation up and checking in with each team member to understand their position, is of paramount importance.

CHECKLIST

Increased productivity ✔

Reduced sickness absenteeism ✔

Reduced turnover ✔

Improved employee satisfaction ✔

Employer of choice status ✔

Develop a solid strategy

To ensure that your approach to employee wellbeing is a solid business investment, your strategy needs to be measured carefully so you can constantly assess the impact it is having. Identifying from the outset what you are trying to achieve, and determining how you can measure it, will be the difference between a successful strategy and a waste of time, money and valuable resources.

Having a clearly defined set of goals, outcomes and metrics is crucial and there are plenty of excellent reporting tools that can be used including HR software and employee surveys. Wellbeing can be seen by some as a bit of an abstract concept; however, once you have established what your anticipated deliverables are, you can present and implement a solid business case and strategy.

Pace your support

The best way to sustain a successful wellbeing programme is to make sure that it is well paced and drip fed throughout the year. This will maintain engagement and, over time, people will start to anticipate what is on offer. Launching all your interventions too soon and all at once can be counterproductive and overwhelming.

Establishing a calendar of events that links to wider awareness days, weeks and months will help you to create structure. This means that you can also tap into any of the free support resources that are often available too. Pace is key to supporting successful wellbeing programmes and sustainable outcomes.

Pacesetting
Leadership

Communicate what is available

Effectively communicating what you have available to support wellbeing is essential. Too often leaders and line managers don't know about the different employee benefit products and why they are useful. Ask yourself the following questions:

1. How are we communicating our benefits package?
2. What opportunities are there to communicate this information on a regular basis?
3. Are we maximising all the opportunities we have available to promote this?
4. How clearly do we explain what is available?
5. How do we measure the response?

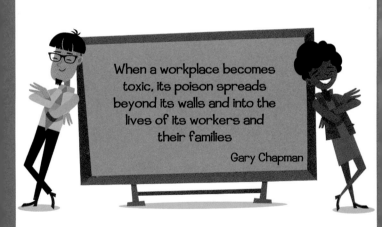

When a workplace becomes toxic, its poison spreads beyond its walls and into the lives of its workers and their families

Gary Chapman

20

Identify and eliminate toxicity

No matter how amazing your wellbeing strategy is, if you have a toxic culture, it will not work. Identifying toxic influences is key and here are a few things to look out for:

- The rumour mill is more powerful than the organisational communication channels
- There is evidence of verbal abuse and bullying
- There is a high rate of employee turnover
- People take credit for work they didn't do
- People play the blame game and don't take responsibility
- There is a culture of discrimination
- Managers don't trust their employees and micromanage
- No-one wants to speak up
- There is a lack of compassion and empathy
- Fun is frowned upon
- Wellbeing initiatives are viewed as tick box exercises

What makes a workplace TOXIC?

People may not remember exactly what you did, or what you said, but they will always remember how you made them feel

Maya Angelou

Manage people well

You may well be familiar with the term 'People don't leave jobs, they leave managers'. It is evident that the way in which managers behave can often be cited as the reason behind employees looking for another job or suffering from work-related stress.

When it comes to leading wellbeing, the line manager's role is pivotal. Some managers lack the necessary 'people management' skills. It is fundamental, therefore, to provide managers with training and support. This will allow line managers to excel in their roles, particularly in support of managing the emotional wellbeing of their teams.

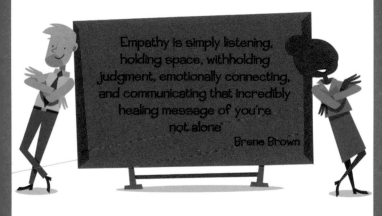

Empathy is simply listening, holding space, withholding judgment, emotionally connecting, and communicating that incredibly healing message of you're not alone'

Brene Brown

Lead with empathy

Leading with empathy is about being sensitive to people's needs, interested in them and their lives, willing to help them with their problems, and being compassionate when they need to share their concerns. Ultimately, it is about demonstrating that you care.

To win the hearts and minds of people, as a leader, it is so important for people to know that you genuinely care and that you are not just paying lip service. It is also worth remembering that you can only truly engage, motivate and influence people when you understand how they feel.

The need for connection and community is primal, as fundamental as the need for air, water, and food

Dean Ornish

Connect and collaborate

Humans have genetically evolved to experience the tangible benefits of human contact, and social connection has been shown to lower anxiety and depression. Being connected also increases feelings of belonging, purpose, happiness, self-worth and confidence. Wellbeing, therefore, depends on our connection and collaboration with others.

The pandemic has disrupted the way that we would normally choose to interact and many people have had to adjust to different ways of connecting and socialising. Establishing and evolving ways to creatively connect people and actively encourage collaboration is essential, and the best way to explore how people want to do this is to ask them what they need and listen to their ideas and suggestions.

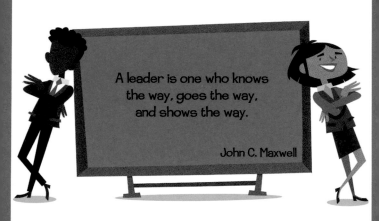

A leader is one who knows
the way, goes the way,
and shows the way.

John C. Maxwell

Champion wellbeing

Leading by example is one of the most powerful and important things that you can do as a leader. When you are seen to be committed to your own wellbeing, from taking regular breaks to adhering to out-of-hours email policies, you are making it acceptable for others to do the same. This will ultimately set the benchmark for self-care amongst your people.

Look for opportunities to raise awareness of what people are doing for their wellbeing and encourage the sharing of best practice and successes. Actively encouraging the role of "Wellbeing Champions" can also be a great way to get more people involved and motivated.

Improve stress intelligence

Burnout is a state of emotional, physical and mental exhaustion caused by excessive and prolonged stress. This often happens when people feel overwhelmed, emotionally drained and unable to meet constant demands. Being aware of stress levels, and raising awareness around stress intelligence, is essential.

There are many ways that people can learn to prioritise self care, establish a healthy lifestyle and manage everyday energy. Assessing organisational culture and processes, as well as offering wellbeing support, will mitigate the damage of mismanaged stress levels.

Encourage breaks and holidays

People stockpiling holidays is something that leaders need to be aware of and monitor. Actively encouraging employees to take holidays, and regular breaks from work, will go a long way towards helping them reduce their stress levels and to be more productive.

As some people adjust to home working, they may feel compelled to work longer hours and take fewer days off, which will impact on their overall wellbeing. You will also need to make sure that you are setting a positive example for them to follow.

Embrace flexible and agile working

One of the ways to support wellbeing is to positively embrace and implement flexible working hours. This has proven to be one of the most effective ways to encourage a healthy life balance, and the option to work flexibly can benefit those who have childcare or family commitments.

Many people are also now working from home and agile working is becoming the norm. Checking in with remote workers on a regular basis and creating communication channels that help to keep people connected, is key. This will support people's mental health and help you to understand and gauge the stress levels within your teams.

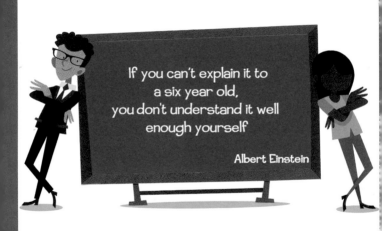

If you can't explain it to
a six year old,
you don't understand it well
enough yourself

Albert Einstein

Communicate with clarity

Keeping things as clear and simple as possible will have a big impact on people's wellbeing and reduce information anxiety. When communication is complicated and confusing, it can add to already heightened stress levels.

Helping people to understand exactly what is being asked of them, and why it matters in the grand scheme of things, is an important approach to take. In times of uncertainty and constant change, it will also be helpful to break things down into manageable tasks. This stops people from feeling overwhelmed and will help them to prioritise better.

Trust and empower

Trust is the glue that holds relationships together. Building trust helps people to be open and receptive to new experiences and, in turn, makes life richer and more interesting.

Empowering people is an important part of the modern day leader's role. When people are micromanaged, it shows a lack of confidence in their abilities and, indeed, a lack of trust. This can be very confining and frustrating and lead to unnecessary and avoidable stress as well as impacting on morale.

Support continual learning

Learning something new every day is one of the greatest joys of being alive as well as having a positive impact on wellbeing. Encouraging curiosity will help people to cultivate a growth mindset and promote a desire for continuous learning.

Providing people with a wide variety of stimulating learning opportunities will encourage personal growth and keep teams engaged and energised.

What you love

PASSION

MISSION

What
you are
good at

IKIGAI

What
the world
needs

PROFESSION

VOCATION

What you can be
paid for

Lead with purpose

A sense of life-meaning and purpose is fundamental to overall wellbeing and is something that can support resilience through challenging times. Leading with purpose means that not only do you have a purpose, but that you can also inspire others to define theirs. One interesting way to explore purpose and meaning is through "Ikigai" which is a Japanese concept that means "a reason for being".

Ikigai is the union point of four fundamental components of life: passion, vocation, profession and mission. The word refers to having a direction or purpose that helps to make life worthwhile and guides people towards taking actions which increases satisfaction and promotes a sense of meaning to life. Ikigai is well worth exploring.

You never know when a
moment and a few sincere words
can have an impact on a life

Zig Zaglar

Celebrate success

One of the best and easiest ways to boost people's overall wellbeing and morale is to show them that you value and appreciate them. This is about recognising hard work and achievements. Recognition plays a large part in employee satisfaction and leaders who take time to celebrate success and say "thank you" will boost morale, strengthen teamwork and make work a much happier place to be.

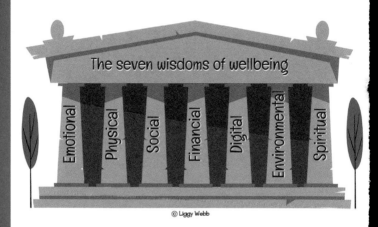

The seven wisdoms of wellbeing

Emotional Physical Social Financial Digital Environmental Spiritual

© Liggy Webb

42